Avery Finn says Goodbye

by Kristina Daniels

Copyright © 2023 Kristina L. Daniels.

All rights reserved. This book or any portion thereof may not be reproduced or used in any manner whatsoever without the express written permission of the publisher except for the use of brief quotations in a book review.

Printed through PublisherDrive and its book distributers.

First printing, 2023.

KLDAZllc
Alb., NM 87112
United States

www.KristinaLDaniels.com

Forward

This book, Avery Finn says Goodbye, was inspired by true life events. Avery had only been in my care a year when my older cat, Dixie, was diagnosed with renal failure. I wrote the ending to this story to process my own grief, and imagined the ending in a way I wish things had gone. Death is a such an important part of our lives and can be a beautiful end to a story. I believe that as families and communities, we should talk about death more in order to normalize its natural role in the cycle of life. Thank you to my Aunt Mary J., who edited this "tail". Thank you to all my beloveds for escorting me on this amazing journey, especially Dixie, Avery & Kaya, Benni & Meg, Sophie, Cassie & Tad.

Kristina

Hi, my name is Avery Finn. I am a three-year-old cat with a handsome coat of grey and white fur. I am adopted and live with another cat named Ms. Dixie. We live with our human companion who takes care of us.

I love Dixie and I love my human mistress, but what I love most in this world is the great outdoors! I like the smell of the green grass and soaking myself in the sunlight. I am very good at hunting birds and even lizards!

If you are looking for me, try searching the tree branches, or you might find me rolling in the dirt turning my fur dusty brown. My human mistress tries to keep me inside, "for my own good," but I have discovered my own secret ways to get outside and have had a number of great adventures!

The adventure I am going to share with you today makes me feel sad, but I still think it is an adventure worth sharing. This is a story about saying goodbye to my friend Dixie.

My favorite time of day is morning. I wake up my sleepy family by "me-owing" really loudly until my human opens her bedroom door and picks me up, and then slings me over her shoulder. I like to stay perched, purring on her shoulder, then jump off and race to everyone to the kitchen.

This morning, when I raced to the kitchen my friend Dixie was not up. She was still lying on her bed instead of racing with me. She meows softly when she sees me. I come closer, sniff her and try to lick her nose, but she growls. So I back away and look over my shoulder at the stairs waiting for our human to come and make Dixie get up.

When our human sees Dixie, she kneels down beside her. She touches Dixie's nose and looks into her eyes. "Dixie, do you want some breakfast?" We both look at Dixie, but she meows quietly and sounds like she is very tired. My mistress walks out of the room, and I hear her talking on the phone. After she hangs up the phone, she comes back over to Dixie and me. She says she is taking Dixie to the Veterinarian. A Veterinarian is a doctor who takes care of sick animals.

Dixie hides her head down in her chest. I don't think Dixie is feeling very well.

My human feeds me breakfast, and before I finish, she packs Ms. Dixie into the cat carrier and disappears. I finish up my breakfast, then jump up and look out my favorite window to search for birds. I see a couple that I can frighten, and flick my tail back and forth to scare them. Today, they don't seem to notice me, so I sit up and put my paws against the window. I stand as tall as I can on my back legs and yell "ME-OOOOWW," but the birds don't move.

I feel angry with them for not paying attention to me. Then I feel a bit scared, because I am also thinking about Dixie and the Veterinarian. I wonder if she is okay. I worry she will have to get a shot. I hate shots, even when my human says I am brave. Thinking about the doctor makes me feel small and worried, so I lie down next to Dixie's bed and take a nap.

I wake up when I hear the door open. Dixie sounds pretty upset. She is talking through the cat carrier, and when she is put down, she runs out of the carrier right to her bed. I sit next to her, and she lets me lick her forehead fur.

Ms. Dixie is sick. My mistress takes care of her by changing her food. She gets wet food instead of dry kibbles and she has to take medicine. After the medicine, my friend feels better and sometimes we even play.

After a couple of weeks of taking the medicine, I notice Dixie just wants to watch the birds. She seems tired all day and all night. One day she decides not to take her medicine and runs away when she hears our human getting the medicine ready. When our human sees that Dixie is hiding, she asks Dixie what she wants. When the talk is over, my human is crying.

Things change after the talk. Dixie gets to eat as much salmon as she wants. I tell my mistress that I want salmon, too, but she doesn't give it to me as often as Dixie.

One day, after we both ate a helping of salmon, I try to start a game of tag, but Dixie says she is too tired to play with me anymore. She talks about going away, but won't tell me where she is going.

This makes me feel sad and angry and confused. Sometimes I feel all of these things at once. Once I swatted at Dixie because I felt angry that she was leaving and I didn't know what to do or say. My feelings are heavy inside my body and feel yucky. Dixie feels bad. Our human says she feels bad, too. So we all feel bad together.

I hang out upstairs in my room to stay out of everyone's way. Dixie has an upset tummy and throws up a lot. One night, she gets sick and crawls under our mistress's bed. Then she says she doesn't want to come out.

The next day, the doorbell rings and I race downstairs to see who it is.

It is the Veterinarian! I jump up onto the couch, afraid the doctor might be here to give me a shot. But my human says, "Avery, the doctor isn't here for you. " She lets the Veterinarian into our house. Then, my human brings Dixie downstairs in her arms. She puts Dixie in her bed and pets her until she settles down. I am very scared and sit next to my human and Dixie, and lick my human's hand.

The Veterinarian comes over and sits beside Dixie. After telling Dixie what a nice cat she is, the doctor pokes her with a needle! I jump back because it looked like it hurt, but Dixie doesn't seem to mind.

My human looks at me and has tears in her eyes when she explains that Ms. Dixie is going on a trip and she won't be coming back. She tells me that Dixie's body hurts and Dixie doesn't want to be in pain. She tells me Dixie had decided she was ready to say goodbye the day she stopped taking her medicine. She says that even though Dixie is going away, she will always be with us, only in our hearts from this day on. I try to tell her I don't want Dixie to leave, that my heart already hurts.

Then I look at my friend, and Dixie looks so tired and sad. I don't want my friend to hurt any more. So I say goodbye and tell her how much I will miss her and wish her a good trip. I tell her that I hope there are lots of birds to watch where she is going. Then I leave the room and go upstairs to my own very soft bed, curl up and cry myself to sleep.

The next day, I woke up with sunlight streaming through the window. I flex my paws before rolling out of bed and then bathe myself, to be sure my fur is handsomely groomed. I begin my morning "me-owwws," and my human finds me and picks me up. Slinging me over her shoulder, she hugs me close.

She is crying. I try to jump down because she is squeezing me too hard, but she holds me tighter. We walk toward the stairs, and then I remember that Dixie won't be waiting for us. My heart begins to feel very large and heavy. I lean in closer to my human, hugging her as we walk down the stairs together.

The End.

Are you a fan of Avery Finn?

Find more about Avery Finn and his adventures on the author's website, kristinaLdaniels.com.

Avery Finn also has a social media presence on YouTube
@adventuresofaveryfinn
&
TikTok@averyfinn1

Do you read books on an electronic device?

Check out Avery Finn's eBooks

A Note from the Author

Dear Reader, saying goodbye to a beloved is difficult. One of the ways I found comfort after Ms. Dixie died was through writing. Sometimes when I wrote, I was trying to make sense of her death, other times I was trying to rewrite the ending of her life. Writing in my journal and eventually speaking my feelings was a part of process for letting go. This is called a grieving process. Folks call it a process because letting go is more than one step, one practice or action.

If you were to write a goodbye story, what would it be about?

There are some blank pages here, and this is an invitation to begin.

www.ingramcontent.com/pod-product-compliance
Lightning Source LLC
Chambersburg PA
CBHW070051070426
42449CB00012BA/3236